WRITING KILLER COVER COPY

INDIE INSPIRATION BOOK 2

ELANA JOHNSON

AEJ
CREATIVE WORKS

CHAPTER ONE: ELANA JOHNSON IS ELANA JOHNSON AND NO ONE ELSE

Hello! I'm Elana Johnson, a multiple USA Today bestselling author, Amazon bestselling author, Kindle All-Star Author, and have been making six-figures with my writing since 2016.

I taught at my first writing conference in 2009, and helping other authors along their journey is something I'm passionate about. It's something I've been recognized for, and it's something I hope to be able to keep doing.

I started writing in 2007, and the first Kindle device was introduced in November of that same year. Self-publishing was not the thing it is now, all these years later.

If you had written a book and you wanted it published, there were several places online to look for information on small publishers that took unagented submissions, as well as literary agents.

I'd written a book, and I wanted it published, so I waded

into the information that was available, and I started hanging out where writers hang out. There were two places at the time—QueryTracker had (and still does have) an excellent forum. And MySpace.

That's right. MySpace.

Some of you might not even remember MySpace, but I do! I had a profile there, and it was full of all my awesome book stuff.

I distinctly remember a conversation I had at another forum-like website started by the founder of QueryTracker, RallyStorm. Basically RallyStorm is Reddit now, but not done by the same person.

Anyway, we had a writers forum there, and I remember asking if I needed to join Facebook in 2009. Facebook had been around for a few years, but it had just come on the scene for writers and businesses.

I joined, of course. I've pretty much joined anything and everything out there!

Aaaand, I've digressed.

The reason I started telling you all of this is because I jumped into learning how to get an agent and get a publisher. I became an admin at QueryTracker and I, along with a few other ladies, rejuvenated their defunct blog and wrote for them for years.

One of my most popular skills was how to write a query letter. This is the first form of communication you have with an agent or a publisher. It basically does two things: Tells them how awesome your book is and entices them to request to read more.

I've taken those skills and that knowledge and that goal for the query letter and translated it to writing killer cover copy (also known as blurbs) for my Indie publishing.

Think about it. Your blurb on your sales page needs to tell readers how awesome your book is and entice them to "request" to read it. They "request" by buying it or downloading it in Kindle Unlimited.

If you lose them at any point, the answer is no. Agents and editors don't request. Readers don't buy.

So our job as authors writing cover copy/blurbs—and I'll use those two terms interchangeably throughout this book—is to entice readers to one-click buy. Right now. Drop everything they're doing, forget to pick up the kids, burn dinner, and buy our book.

Not only buy it now, but read it *right now*.

Forget about that other book they have on their Kindle, they've not got yours!

That's the dream, isn't it?

Well, let's go make the dream happen!

Okay, wait. More backstory, AKA it's time to be you and stop apologizing for it:

I've been in the business through ups, downs, curves, pits, and more. I started in traditional publishing and have had four literary agents sell my work from here to France, in audio, paper, and ebook formats.

I've written for Hallmark. I've worked with editors from four publishing houses. I've had big deals and highs, and low lows and slumps.

Through it all, I kept writing.

I entered the self-publishing scene in 2014 as a "screw it" way to tell my publisher they'd be upset they passed on my book. No lie. As if they cared. LOL.

But *I* cared, and I wanted to write what I wanted to write.

Go back and read that line again. In today's marketplace, it's all about writing to market. I do that...and I don't. I write what *I* want to write. This was a lesson I learned in 2013, when Simon & Schuster wanted a book similar to the young adult dystopian trilogy I'd already sold to them. So I gave them that. And they passed on it because...it was TOO similar to the YA dystopian trilogy I'd already sold to them.

I was like, SCREW IT. Some of you might use more colorful language.

But that defining moment in my career turned me to self-publishing, and I now only write what I want to write.

I believe there are a lot of ingredients for success in Indie Publishing. Reading this book might be one of them for you.

Ultimately, you'll see a lot of people out there with very loud voices saying that you have to do X, Y, and Z to be successful. But that's *their* version of success, that follows *their* work ethic and *their* personality and *their* home life, and *their their their*.

What's yours?

I think I can write what I want to write *and* write to market. I think I can cover my book well. I think I can write killer cover copy for it. Ad copy. Newsletter copy. All of it.

Isn't that what writers do? We write?

Why is blurb writing so much harder than novel writing?

Here's a secret: It's not.

It's all in your head.

And today, you're going to get out of your head and inside mine. Wait. That doesn't sound right. Haha!

It's pretty freaky in here. But I think one of the reasons I'm able to move fluidly from one thing to another, seemingly without any hitches, is because of two things:

1. I am continually learning. I read a lot of articles. I read a lot of Facebook groups. I lurk quietly, always absorbing. I'm like that sponge sitting next to the sink... Nope. Nope, I'm not that. ;)
2. I take what I learn, and I adapt it to fit...me. Yep. Just me. I tried revising that sentence. Fit my style. Fit my personality. Fit my budget. Yes, yes, and yes.

I do all of that. I've taken a dozen courses on advertising for Indie Authors. I've read dozens of books. I know what I know, but what scares me is what I don't know. I simply don't know what I don't know.

But I believe I can learn.

And when I do, I'm going to take the information provided, and I'm going to make it fit – ME. My style of writing. My genre. My price point. My budget. My personality. My marketing system. All of me. Me, me, me.

I think sometimes, too many people try to do what someone else has done with success, and they end up failing. Or thinking that what that person told them to do was Bad Advice. Or that there's somehow a unicorn out there in them thar woods, and they just can't find it.

(I actually believe there *is* a unicorn, and no, I haven't found it yet.)

Back in the traditional publishing days, I had a good friend named Beth Revis. Some of you might know her. She was writing YA science fiction, and so was I. Our books sold to major publishers about the same time.

I basically stalked Beth. There, I admitted it. I signed up for her newsletter. I went to her website. I read her blog. Anything Beth was doing, I wanted to do too. We were in the same genre. Our books came out within months of each other. Everything looked so good on paper.

The truth was, and I learned very quickly, I couldn't be Beth.

She is a wonderful, fantastic person I still listen to on IG TV.

But I am not Beth.

I will never be Beth.

I cannot do what Beth does and have the same success. I mean, she launched her freaking book into space, you guys! SPACE.

There is no way on this planet I could even come close to being Beth or doing what she did.

Is all lost?

Should I have quit those many long years ago?

Absolutely not.

You're you, and there's no one like you. I'm me, and there's no one like me. I can do some things that you might not be able to. You can do things I can't do.

The point of all of this?

Learn as much as you can from those around you who you deem to be "doing things right."

And then adapt them. Make them fit within the framework of your business, and your personality.

If you do that, you'll find the success you want.

Okay, *now* we're ready to start mastering cover copy!

2

CHAPTER TWO: WHY KILLER COPY IS LIKE THE BILLY GOATS GRUFF

W riting good copy for your products is one of the most essential skills out there. In today's landscape, we don't sit down and read paragraphs about something like we used to. Catalogs are almost a thing of the past, though I'll admit, I like leafing through the Ikea catalog when it shows up!

But we don't need loads of text to sell a product. You need the *right* text. There's a reason Twitter contests are popular with 140 characters and Amazon only gives you 150 characters for the ad copy in their advertising platform.

You need to be able to fit a compelling hook into a short space.

Your cover copy should do three things:

1. Hook a reader to either one-click buy or read on.
2. Tell about your book once you've captured interest to read on.
3. Convince the audience by the end of the copy to buy and read *right now*.

After all, if you're spending your precious time, money, and energy to get people to look at your book, you don't want to lose them with something you have **ultimate** control over.

We'll talk about the hook and a tagline coming up. I'll give you all the parts you need to tell readers about your books too. And hopefully, by the end you've marched them up a mountain, left them there, and they're eagerly one-clicking to buy and read your book.

You are the Billy Goats Gruff. You know, the nursery rhyme about the goats going up the mountain to get fat? And they have to pass the troll under the bridge along the way?

Your cover copy better get you all the way to the top of the mountain—and that's where you'll leave your readers. They'll be salivating to one-click buy, and they won't even know they've taken a ride on a goat.

But you will.

So let's get ready to goat!

Uh, that's not right.

But you know what I mean.

3

WRITING KILLER COVER COPY

I wrote this book because I think every piece of copy I read (or write) can be improved. We're using our cover copy to sell books, and we're writers. So it should get just as much attention, revision, and editing as our full-length novels.

This book is not about writing said novel. I'm assuming you have that step done. Edited, revised, critiqued by trusted readers. No, this book is about what to do *after* you've written the novel—because sometimes the task of writing a blurb for a book can seem twice as daunting as actually writing a book!

So roll up your sleeves. I already know you're a hard worker if you've written a novel. Now let the real fun begin —selling it.

Good back cover copy has four parts, in my opinion.

Each part builds on the one before it, carefully leading the reader up the mountain to get fat on your novel.

Wait, I think *you* might be the one getting fat off the royalties... Unsure about that. The point is, there's a reason some blurbs fall flat. By the end of this book, you'll know what that is and be able to combat it in your own cover copy.

So let's go back to my traditional days. It was 2008, and I had written a book and I wanted to query agents with it. I hadn't heard of Kindle Direct Publishing, though Wikipedia tells me Amazon launched it when they launched their first Kindle.

I didn't know anyone doing it, either digitally or in print—and in fact, in traditional publishing, the whole ebook revolution took that industry by storm. They're still burning from all the lightning strikes in that storm, but that is not a topic for this book.

So it was get an agent, have them sell the book to a publishing house, sail off to your new private island that you could buy with the advance.

Or something like that. LOL.

To do all of that, I needed a query letter, and I was determined to have the very best one I could.

For our purposes, I'm going to take all I've learned about writing the book part of the query letter—because there are other parts to a query that we don't need as Indie publishers —and call it cover copy or a blurb.

All of the principles are the same. All of them. I need to compel a reader (agent) to read what my book is about, getting them excited and dying to read more. Then they buy (or an agent requests to read more).

When I was querying, I had astronomical request rates. At the time, a good request rate was 10%, meaning you'd send 10 queries and get 1 request. I had a 40% request rate, querying over 3 novels.

No, my first novel did not get represented or sold. I've gotten more rejections than pretty much anyone on the planet. It's okay. I'm still breathing. Sometimes.

Anyway, moving on. I was good at writing query letters. I operated a business doing it for other people for a few years. In this book, I'm going to change the word query to cover copy or blurb, and we won't talk about those extraneous parts of a query letter you don't need on your product page.

Okay?

Okay.

Let's go!

Slow and steady wins the race.

When I sat down to really learn how to write cover copy, I had several successful examples in front of me. I'd printed them out, and I spread them out along my counter. I made notes on what the first line was. The second. How many paragraphs it had.

I also had them in digital format, so I could count the

words. I looked at the last paragraph, if there were questions or not, all of it.

Then I started writing my own blurb—by hand, if you can believe it! I'd identified some common themes among successful blurbs, and I believe they still work to this day. There's something intrinsic about them that appeals to readers—and gets them excited to buy.

And don't we want them to buy?

I know I do!

Your cover copy is the bulk of the query letter. It was the first step through the door to an agent and then an editor. Those agents and editors would make judgements about the quality of your writing simply from the quality of your query.

And you know what?

Readers do too. I whispered that in my head, so hopefully you did too.

But seriously, in a normal voice now, readers do too. We all make mistakes and have typos and all of that. This isn't bashing anyone—because here's a funny story. Well, it's funny now.

When I released Writing and Releasing Rapidly, another of my Indie Inspiration titles, I was scared out of my mind. But excited. I had checked everything 5000 times.

And you know what?

The cover had a typo on it.

THE COVER IMAGE.

I'd showed it to my friends, my husband, my designer

had sent multiple versions to me. None of us saw it.

So embarrassing.

We all make mistakes. But what I'm saying is this: If you're not satisfied with your cover copy (or you know, if your cover has a typo on it), fix it.

See if you can't get your sales and conversions on ads to go up because of it. I think you will, because readers are also making judgements on the quality of your writing before they even buy your book. Don't give them a reason to click somewhere else.

Impress them.

Writing cover copy is the same as penning a novel. I have a personal philosophy for this, in today's current Indie Publishing Climate (IPC).

It's three-fold. In order to gain more fans, you need to do three things:

1. Make your book *look* like a bestseller
2. Make it *sound* like a bestseller
3. Write the very best book you can

The first one has to do with the cover. Your book should LOOK LIKE other books out there that are already selling well. Now, don't go all cray-cray and literally use the same cover models and fonts and all of that. We're not in the plagiarism business.

But it should look like a duck and quack like a duck if you're trying to sell a duck.

Right?

Quack, quack.

The second part of that references the cover copy, or the blurb. If my book looks like it fits nicely in the genre, I need to make sure it *sounds* like it too. Now, you may have heard there are only seven story ideas or something like that. I'm not telling you to copy plots.

I'm telling you to do some research and see what others in your genre are doing with their blurbs. First person? Third person? Questions? No questions? Long? Short? Bold type? Capital tagline? Etc.

Number three is subjective, and you actually have no idea if you're hitting that or not, because readers determine what they like and what they deem "good". I aim to write the best book I can. Edit it well. Cover it nicely. Make it look like and sound like other authors in my genre who I can see are selling well.

Then, all I can do is hope and pray that the words inside my book resonate with a reader. If they do, they'll come back to me over and over again. And that's how a fan is made.

We do the same with our blurbs—they're an essential tool in our selling arsenal. So write the best cover copy you can. Get it critiqued. Make it better. Edit it. Perfect it.

Sell more books with it.

So are you ready to do that?

Let's do it!

4

THE TAGLINE

A tagline can also be called a logline. You might hear that term more often in the film industry, and almost all publishers and anyone trying to get you to consume media uses them.

You're trying to get a reader to consume your media, therefore, you need to be good at writing taglines too.

These are the short, hooky sentences you'll see a lot of Indies put in bold right at the top of their book description pages. It's worth your time and energy to sit down and work on the very best taglines you can. Test different ones and see which ones convert best. Use those. We'll talk more about testing in a little bit.

A tip here though: I try to make my taglines less than 150 characters. Not always, but sometimes. Why? That's what Amazon lets me use in my ad copy, and I've seen it help my conversions to have the same tagline in my ad that's on my product page.

So remember, I'd trained myself to write query letters, and I was really good at it. I had a thriving business writing query letters for other people, and I wrote entire blog series on how to craft the best query letter out there. I've taught classes and workshops from California to Kansas on writing killer blurbs or writing a killer query letter, or whatever the title of the class needed to be for the conference where I was presenting.

When I turned to Indie Publishing in 2014, I realized all of my query letter writing skills would continue to serve me—and now you!—well.

See, I wrote a line in my query letter for a book that Simon & Schuster would go on to publish. It was "Control or be controlled." It was the last line in my query letter—the consequence (which we'll talk more about later on).

And that line—those four words—made it through the scads of people who work on a book in traditional publishing to the cover.

The *cover*.

The tagline *I* wrote was now the tagline on the front cover of my book. The traditional market doesn't even keep titles, people. They keep NOTHING an author comes up with on their own. Literally.

And yet...my tagline made it through all the chopping blocks. All the agents. All the editors. All the vice-presidents. All the art department designers.

That's how powerful your taglines can and should be. It's worth the time to get them right.

Your tagline should be something that entices a reader to one-click buy. Or entices a reader to keep reading, just in case they're still on the fence.

On Amazon, you only get a few lines "above the fold." If you look at a series page, you get two lines for each book. I made some of my taglines shorter and in all caps, and they look really nice on those series pages. Check out an example here—just scroll down and read the capitalized, bold taglines.

What both of these things mean is there's a "See More" link on each individual product page, and you want to put your best stuff *above* that, enticing readers to buy without having to make that extra click and read more.

You can and should still entice them to buy the book if they do click that See More link. Every word should take them further and further up the mountain toward buying. Remember those goats? You have to get them past the trolls.

Here's my formula for taglines:

1. List character.
2. Use common tropes in plain language.
3. Spell out the conflict in one succinct sentence.

That's it. Surprisingly simple, right? Haha. Right. You can exercise your tagline muscles by looking at bestsellers in your categories. What are they doing for taglines? What do their blurbs look like? Are they in first person or third? Are they long or short? Do they use a lot of questions or not?

First: List character.

So when you sit down to work on some taglines, you're going to start with character. Answer: *Who is the main character?*

Write a couple of words for them, thinking of tropes. Female detective? Cowboys? Billionaires? Amateur sleuth? Shifter?

Be smart. Use the tropes within characters you know are selling books. Not yours—yet—but look at what IS selling and see what they're doing.

I'll put in a word of caution here, as I'm not the first to say, "Go to Amazon and see what the bestsellers are doing."

That's good advice.

BUT – you have to understand something. They're bestsellers. They're selling a lot of books. Usually, when you're at a point like this in your career, it doesn't really matter what you're doing. Your name is selling the book.

I'm going to say that again, because I think it's really important. Usually, when authors are at a point where they are consistent bestsellers, *it doesn't really matter what they're doing*. Their name is selling the book.

So. That said, you can look at some bestsellers and see them doing things differently. And you might think those things are working, but really, they're only working because of the name already on the front cover.

Be sure to be smart. Look at *a lot* of books across your genre. Go up to the Top 10 in your category and start there. Look at 10 – 50, and see what *they're* doing. Is it the same as #1? It might be. It might not be.

Another thing to try is to identify an author that you think your books are very much like. The covers are similar. Genre is a match. And you want to get their readers to read your books. What are *they* doing?

See if you can do it too.

Okay, so you're starting with character. Putting in a trope with the character if you can. Here's a couple of examples: A cowboy with a son

A witch who can't do simple spells

A former football star

Can you see how I'm using tropes *and* identifying character? These provide meta-data words (cowboy, witch, football) that tell readers what kind of CHARACTER they'll get while also identifying tropes (single dad, sports star, paranormal).

STOP and WORK: Take a few minutes and write down

five character-based beginnings for your tagline. Tap them out on your phone. Type them up in a blank email—that's what I would do! LOL.

And don't worry! I didn't leave you high and dry. You can download a 2-page PDF file that has all 5 parts of a killer blurb that you can print and use to your heart's content! It's got room for notes and attempts and your thoughts.

Go grab it here.

Up next: Use common tropes in plain language.

If you have a second chance romance, you better be using those three words. Fake fiancé? Get it in there. Psychological thriller? Space opera? Whatever it is, it should be clearly identified.

Hopefully within the title, subtitle, or series name, which is in bold by the cover, but also in the description box —specifically in the tagline. If you do the work, you can get it in there.

A cowboy with a son, his old high school girlfriend, and their second chance at love.

There's a tagline that spells out character and trope in very plain language. It doesn't take many words—and remember, you don't *have* many words to use. The shorter and pithier your taglines are, the better.

And that one is 85 characters, so I know it's going to fit in the Amazon ads box. I can even add: *Second chance romance!* And *Read today!* I still have 30 characters to spare, and bam. My ad copy is done too.

I mean, might as well be knocking birds out left and right while I'm working on this tagline stuff, right?

The tagline is something readers can zip through as they navigate to the buy button. It becomes something you can use in your advertising. Then, when people click on your ad and they're taken to your product page, it matches. They know they're in the right spot, and they're primed to buy.

Up next: Spell out the conflict.

I know, I hear some of you saying, "I have to get the conflict in the tagline? That's impossible!"

It is, and it isn't. You don't have to go deep. But you should hint at what readers will get before you launch into the full blurb/description. You can say a lot with a few words, and the better you are at that, the better you'll be at writing not only copy, but books too.

You can combine the conflict with the tropes, with the characters. In fact, the best taglines do.

Here's an example from one of my bestselling books: *A wounded Army cowboy, a divorcée with a child, and their second chance to heal old hurts...*

I don't tell you want the hurts are. But I have two characters (this is obviously a romance), defined in tropes (cowboy, military hero, single mom), and their conflict—an old flame that burned them both, which now they get a second chance to have.

You don't have to go super deep. But if I have a reader who likes cowboys, Army heroes, or single moms, I've got them hooked already. If I have a reader who loves second chance romance, they know they'll get one here.

Those first few words, which I would recommend you put in bold in your descriptions, can do so much to sell your books.

NOTE: Your blurb and cover WORK TOGETHER to convince a reader to buy. They should both speak to genre, character, and conflict so readers can make split-second judgments. That's the society we live in now. Split-second judgments.

Quack, quack.

Make it *look like* and *sound like* something familiar but also unique.

So while this book isn't about covers, you should make sure yours is as to-market as you can get it. Don't be afraid to recover if necessary. I recently did this for a series that was floundering and it's doing much better now.

Once you have your tagline down, you can test it. I'm almost to that. Then you just need to focus on the rest of your blurb/description, which you can nail flawlessly in the next few chapters.

. . .

Testing Taglines:

I think there is great power in testing. I know it takes time. It can take money. You might fail. All three of those prevent people from achieving their best results. I know, because I've tried to cut corners on pretty much everything in Indie Publishing.

I never said I was perfect! I also regret nothing I've done. That sounds super arrogant, I'm sure. I don't mean it to be.

What I mean it to be is this: You don't know what you don't know. Sure, you can read books and take courses and lurk in groups the way I have—and still do. But until you try a strategy for yourself—*your* books, *your* genre, *your* personality—you do not know what will truly work *for you*.

So yes, I've made a lot of mistakes, but I've learned from them. I know for myself what works well, and I know what doesn't. If I keep doing more of what works and less of what doesn't, I should be able to find some measure of success.

In the end, it's only when I test that I find success. What works for one person—even with a very similar book—might not work for you. Remember Beth? Don't be Beth. Be you!

You need to test.

The simplest and cheapest way to test taglines is with Amazon Advertising (formerly Amazon Marketing Services).

Create a Sponsored Product ad and use their custom text option. There, you get 150 characters for a tagline. I've put in my top 5 taglines on the exact same keyword list (only test one thing at a time, and we're testing taglines here, not audiences), set the ads at $5/day each, and waited a week.

Some of you might be dying about this. That's $175, you say!

Well, kind of. Amazon's not generally going to spend all of that. After the 7 days, you should have some good data on which tagline seems to be working the best.

Use that one.

You can change your description on Amazon any time you want. You might be surprised which tagline converts best, and you'll probably find that different taglines convert better with different audiences.

That's why you test them.

You can do the same with Facebook, and I often do. Facebook, however, *will* spend all of your money. It's like they do it as easily as breathing. So if you set a $5/day budget on Facebook, they WILL spend it.

The difference is, Facebook gives you results a lot faster than Amazon does. I've found, however, that I need to let my $5/day Facebook ads run for 2-3 days before I have ENOUGH data.

Now, you could up the ad spend and get the data faster, but then you're spending more. It's all up to you.

Just be sure you're only testing one thing—the tagline— however you decide to do it. Facebook gets a little convoluted, because there are images besides the cover involved, and yeah.

Once you've done some testing, you can update your

tagline to the best one, perhaps changing it up every now and then as the market changes, or as you start advertising to new audiences.

FINAL WORDS ON TAGLINES:

- List character, trope, and conflict as succinctly as possible.
- Write down 5 taglines for the same book and edit/rework them until you're happy with one. Get feedback from friends/other writers on it.
- Test the tagline on Amazon or Facebook advertising.
- Make it stand out. You can use bold or even bigger letters. Kindleprenuer has a great formatting tool here.
- Don't be afraid to change your tagline at any time, as the market changes or as your tests indicate.

5

WRITING GREAT BLURBS, PART 1: THE HOOK

I think learning how to write cover copy is one of the most valuable skills you can have. I learned by doing it by hand. I made notes. I think and think and think, and then I post my copy for critique.

I still do this with every book I publish.

I think everyone needs their person. You know, like on Grey's Anatomy, Meredith has Christina as her person?

You need one of those. Because you're going to be showing some seriously bad cover copy to this person, and you don't want it to come back and bite you later!

My person is Bonnie Paulson. We have a blurb chat in Slack where we can post our blurbs and get feedback on them.

So get a person. And be sure to get some feedback on your blurbs, even if it's sending out different taglines in your newsletter and asking people what they like better. They'll tell you! Now, whether you should listen to them is an entirely different story.

That's why we all need a Bonnie in our lives.

Remember how I sat down with several successful versions of cover copy? Spread them out and made notes? Well, during all of that, I identified these four essential parts of killer cover copy:

1. The Hook
2. The Setup
3. The Conflict
4. The Consequence

Once I could physically see this formula, everything came together for me. I'm a very visual learner, so this was tremendously helpful.

Note: Cover copy should be written in the tone of your novel. Keep that in mind as you go through this studying process. Just because someone else's successful copy is over-the-top funny doesn't mean yours will be—unless you've also written a comedy. Remember this, but the copy-writing formula doesn't change because of it.

· · ·

Up first, the Hook.

I think you need a hook, and sometimes this can be the tagline. In fact, for most of us, it's going to be that bolded tagline we worked on in the last chapter. That doesn't mean all of our work is done, though.

Every other sentence in the blurb should lead someone higher up the mountain. Man, I've talked about goats and ducks so much in this book! I'll try to take that down a notch. Maybe step up the Grey's Anatomy references. Time will tell.

Your hook should:

1. Sum up the novel in one sentence.
2. Propel the reader to read the rest of the cover copy with interest.

Notice I didn't say it should make me gasp. It shouldn't make me guess at anything either. So many people I've worked with over the years are so worried about spoilers in their blurbs.

People, you don't need to worry about that. What you do need to worry about is losing readers because you're too vague. Nobody wants vagueness. I mean, think about it. Who LOVES a good Vaguebook post? Do you? Do you really??

No.

No one likes those! They frustrate us and make us want to unfollow people who can't simply spell out what they're trying to say.

Don't be Vaguebook. Don't get blocked. Don't get passed over because you can't say what your book is about.

Recently, I watched a movie where a child got lost and his seemingly loving mother never came to get him. It wasn't the point of the movie, but I was fixated on it. Why didn't that mother come back for him? Where was she now? What had happened to her? Would I ever find out? What had the boy done to find out??

On and on. I kept leaning over to my husband and asking him questions, and he was like, *Dude, Elana. Chill. I'm sure we'll find out.*

But I didn't trust the movie to tell me. I was worried about it, and I started looking it up on my phone right there in the movie theater. That's right. I needed to know BEFORE the movie showed me.

If you leave out key parts of your blurb that brand-new readers need to know...they might just click somewhere else. They don't trust you yet, and it's your job to earn that trust.

You do it first in the blurb by carefully putting all the relevant details they need to be satisfied, the exact same way you do in your actual book.

Your hook should sum up the novel and make me want to read more.

Basically, you want your hook to be the answer to the question, "What is your book about?"

You should've seen my panic face the first time I was asked that. I was like, "Well, it's about this guy, and he's kind of immortal...and there's this girl, and she can make him mortal. Or something."

Yeah, it didn't go well. I don't think I gained a fan at the check-out counter at the grocery store. LOL.

In general, I advocate for hooks that:

1. Grab, entice, get out all in one sentence
2. Mimic the tone of your novel
3. Are strong statements, not questions. This one is not a hard and fast rule. But it's generally better to avoid yes/no questions right off the bat.

A hook can be your tagline. It can also be longer, the first sentence of the actual blurb below the tagline. Hooks often name main characters immediately, instead of referring to them as tropes.

STOP and WORK:

Write a hook for your WIP. Right now. I often write my blurbs well before my books are done. Usually right about the Break Into Two, which is at 25% in my novels. Why?

Because everything I need for my blurb has been written. I know the characters (hook). I know what they want (setup). I know why they can't have it (main conflict). And I know what will happen if they don't figure out how to get it (consequence).

I can write the blurb at 25% of the book. Sometimes before that if the concept is really clear in my head.

So take a few minutes and think about the book you're writing right now. If you're already into the second act, take a minute and write a hook for it.

What is your book about? Who's the main character and why should I care about him/her?

Remember you can grab a printable PDF to help you with your blurb! It's here.

Hooks are often longer, and often include names. Here's one for one of my novels: *Darren Buttars is cool, collected, and quiet—and utterly devastated when his girlfriend of nine months, Farrah Irvine, breaks up with him because he wanted her to ride her horse in a parade.*

I give you more information about Darren. We know from the tagline above that he's a cowboy, so I'm not stuffing that trope down your throat again. Instead, I'm giving more about him in as few words as possible. He's not a big talker, and his girlfriend—who I also name—broke up with him over something that shouldn't be a big deal.

Why *is* it a big deal to *her*? Who is she?

I should keep reading to find out. <<I whispered that again, because that's what I want readers to be doing.

They're on the goat, bumping along. And it's my job to creepily whisper to them as they march up the mountain *Keep reading to find out.*

You're going to love this story.

Better buy and read now.

See how hooks do that? The propel. They further entice, past the tagline. They give more information without overwhelming. Because we're going to give readers even more in a minute when we talk about the setup. The hook's job is to keep people going. They're nearing the first bridge, and we don't want them to stop now.

In fact, maybe they should just go buy now. Readers can, and should, be able to stop reading your blurb at any time and *go buy now.* If you put all the pieces in the right places, they'll never have a reason to say no and move on to something else.

Now, they might have landed on your page by accident, so they don't buy. Their toddler may have started screaming right when they looked at your book, so they don't buy. They might not have the money if your book is priced higher than they can afford. *They might, they might, they might.*

But it should never be your cover copy that is deterring them from buying. I've said it before, but I'll say it again:

You have ultimate control over this, and you can make it the best it can be.

So do it!

FINAL WORDS ON HOOKS:

- Do you have a person you can bounce ideas off of? Who can look at your bad copy for you?
- Can you answer: What is your book about?
- Write one sentence that mimics the tone of the novel and springboards the reader to keep reading.
- Be succinct in telling who the characters are to propel readers into the setup.

6

WRITING GREAT BLURBS, PART 2: THE SETUP

A h, the setup. This is the spot where most of you get bogged down. You've arrived at the bridge with the troll under it. You let the troll grab onto one of your goaty hooves, and he rips you from the path that leads to fatness.

But seriously, you do.

Don't allow yourself to get lost in the setup! It does get quite the bulk of you copy, and it's where you deliver on what you just hooked a reader to read. After all, you can't just have a hook and then let everything else go. Well, sometimes you can, but we'll talk about that later.

Following the hook, you need to get to the problem. This requires a little bit of setup. A little bit of backstory, if you will. A few details.

It's not everything and the kitchen sink.

It's not every character you've ever named.

It's not all the cool magic systems you created.

Save all of that for the actual book.

In the cover copy, you need the view the setup like the bridge the billy goats are crossing. It's an essential piece of the story. We can't get from Here to There without it.

But we certainly don't want to spend more time on the troll-infested bridge than we have to. You know?

We just go over it. Quickly. Trip-trap, trip-trap, set us up and move on.

In the setup, you have a few goals:

1. Provide a few details about who your main character is. You've hooked the reader to find out more about your main character, so give them what they want.

2. World-building information if pertinent. For fantasy and science fiction, a little taste of the world would go in the setup section of the blurb. For mystery, horror, thriller or other genres, including the setting here wouldn't be a bad idea.

3. The catalyst that moves the main character into the conflict.

Just like in your writing, what you include in the cover copy should have a purpose for being there. It's not to show off, either. Goats can only run 10 mph at top speed. I Googled how fast trolls could run, but the Internet failed me.

I'm going to say faster than 10 mph.

Don't let your goat show off on the bridge. Get him over it and move on.

In the setup, I advocate for 3-5 sentences, tops. TOPS. That's about 75-100 words. If you can do it in less, great. Those of you writing paranormal or supernatural or something out of this world, you do need to give us some details in the setup about your world.

For those of you writing in contemporary worlds, the social status of things can go a long way toward establishing your world.

In another life, I wrote science fiction and fantasy. Here's the hook and setup for one of my fantasy novels that won the Kindle Scout program and was published by Amazon:

Her voice could unleash a war. (This is the hook. I put it here just to show it to you. It's short. It's pithy. It compels us to read more. I'd actually categorize this as a tagline, not a hook, but that's okay. They're somewhat interchangeable.)

Twenty-three-year-old Echo del Toro doesn't know about the bride-choosing festivities the tyrannical Prince of Nyth has planned—until she's taken from her home by five armed soldiers. She's led under the cover of a magically produced storm to an opulent compound to join hundreds of girls, each vying to be chosen as the next Queen of Nyth.

That's it. This is a very short blurb, but the book is over 100,000 words. I could go on and on. I don't need to.

STOP and WORK:

Think about that book you're writing right now. The one you've written down 5 taglines for. The one you've got a nice, compelling hook for.

Now think of the setup. The imperative characters readers need to know about before buying. The way the world operates. And the catalyst that will move them into the main conflict.

Write a few sentences that has those things in them.

Remember, your cover copy mimics the voice and tone of your novel, so do that here too.

I know! There are SO MANY THINGS to keep straight. But if you work on each piece as you go, you can get an amazing blurb that will sell your books. So it's work worth doing.

In the setup, you need the readers to know who the major players are. You need the readers to know a little bit about the world. You need the readers to know there's something big coming to those characters and that world—the conflict—and you need the readers to know HOW they get to that conflict. That's the catalyst to the conflict.

All fiction is about conflict. If you spend too much time

on the setup, you're robbing the reader of the conflict—and robbing yourself of a sale.

Don't bog us down in too many details.

Don't introduce your entire cast of secondary characters.

Don't try to impress with single sentences that are 65 words long or the cool names of your universe far, far away. Just lay it out.

Do tell us what moves the characters from Here to There. That's the catalyst, and all fiction has catalysts too. If yours doesn't...you have a Houston-we-have-a-problem problem. That's one that resides in your manuscript, not your cover copy.

And bonus! The cover copy can sometimes reveal holes in our actual books! Take it as a bonus, not something to drown yourself in ice cream over. Or both. Eat the ice cream. Then go fix your book. Then fix the cover copy. Then sell it!

Remember, the setup is a bridge in getting up the mountain. It's not the destination—and there are trolls down there.

Trip-trap, trip-trap. Go over it.

FINAL WORDS ON THE SETUP:

- Stick with the main character, introducing a secondary character if necessary.

- Get there quick = 3-5 sentences / 75 – 100 words
- Give only the important details that build character or setting
- Mimic the tone of the novel
- Include the catalyst to the conflict
- Answer the question: What does the character want?

7

WRITING GREAT BLURBS, PART 3: THE CONFLICT

Now that you've hooked your reader and gotten them past the setup, you're to the part everyone wants to read—the conflict. Every novel needs it. In fact, the more conflict, the better.

In the blurb, you want to highlight the main conflict, not every single one in every single chapter. You can't even do that in the synopsis, so don't try.

Let's recap for a moment. Your blurb is about 4 things:

1. Who the main character(s) is/are (Hook)
2. What they want (Setup)
3. Why they can't have it (Main conflict)
4. What will happen if they can't figure out how to get it (Consequence)

We've discussed taglines, hooks, and the setup so far. We're onto the main conflict, and this is going to lay out for the reader what the Big Deal is. It's going to explain to them why they should pause Netflix and read your book instead. Stay up late reading when they have an early-morning meeting.

Conflict drives fiction, and I'd dare to say all entertainment. It's why we consume. *There's conflict here! What's going to happen??*

It's why we slow down and rubberneck at car accidents. It's why we read Internet news and turn on the news when there are hurricanes or school shootings.

What's going to happen? Is everyone all right?

Naturally, as humans, we want everything to be good in the end. We want right to prevail, and Voldemort to "get his," and everyone to be a hero.

I want to be a hero in my own life. I want to win, to prevail, to be the one to survive the zombie apocalypse.

Don't you?

I think it's human nature to want to win and prevail, save the day, and make sure everyone else does too. I mean, unless you're a serial killer. They don't even untuck their sheets to sleep!

For a real-life example of humans enjoying conflict, I go downstairs and work on a puzzle every Monday night. Why? Because *The Bachelorette* is on!

I have to know what's going to happen! There's so much

conflict in that show. SO MUCH. She wants a husband who "gets her." They all want her.

What's in their way?

Pretty much everything, including cameras, Chris, fifteen other guys, her crying, walls, emotional barriers, alcohol, etc. The list could literally go on and on.

You don't need to do that for your cover copy, though.

Here's the tagline for *The Bachelorette*:

One lucky woman. Twenty-five men. Which one will win her heart?

Twenty-five-freaking men. That's some conflict right there.

And don't even get me started on *The Bachelor*, because wow. Women are usually more drama than men. No offense. But yeah. In fact, reality TV is as huge as it is because of the natural conflicts between human beings when placed in extraordinary situations.

And couldn't that basically be a tagline for fiction? Conflict between human beings (or cyborgs, I suppose) when placed in extraordinary situations?

Yes, yes it is.

In our conflict section of our blurb, we're going to be sticking to the main one. The biggest one.

Main conflict [*meyn kon-flikt*]: The central thing that prevents the character from getting what they want.

Note: If you didn't setup what the character wants in the setup, you can do it during the conflict. Sometimes we

can get that in there, and sometimes we can't. Depending on
the genre, sometimes what a character wants is implied.

Here are a couple of examples. The first one is from my
very first traditionally published book. The query letter with
a 40% request rate? That's this one. The one with a consequence statement that made it through billions of people
(hyperbole) to the front cover of my book? This one.

I'm going to include the hook and setup so you can see
it. See if you can pick out the details for each of those pieces
as well. Remember a hook details more about the character.
Often names them and gives me some information about
what type of character I'll get. It also speaks to genre if ages
are included.

And the setup should tell me about the main characters,
the world they live in (doesn't have to be speculative, but can
be), and anything important about secondary characters or
setting I absolutely have to know.

So let's take a look!

Hook: *In a world where Thinkers brainwash the population and Rules are not meant to be broken, fifteen-year-old
Violet Schoenfeld does a hell of a job shattering them to
pieces.*

STOP and THINK: What genre is this? Do you hear me
whispering to keep reading to see what will happen next?

I'll just put that here.

Keep reading to find out what happens next.

LOL.

Setup: *After committing her eighth lame ass crime (walking in the park after dark with a boy, gasp!), Vi is taken to the Green, a group of Thinkers who control the Goodgrounds. She's found unrehabilitatable (yeah, she doesn't think it's a word either) and exiled to the Badlands. Good thing sexy Bad boy Jag Barque will be going too.*

STOP and THINK: Do you see the important characters? This is a YA dystopian novel, by the way. Those often contain a lot of capitalized words. The tone of the book is mimicked in the cover copy—the MC often includes parentheticals in the narrative. There is swearing. There is sarcasm and wit.

Do you see all of that?

There's another character mentioned—he's the male main character. There are elements of her world. There's a catalyst to the conflict—she's arrested and sent away with a sexy bad boy.

Oooh, what will happen next?!

I might have shouted that.

Anyway, let's look at the conflict part of the blurb.

Conflict: *Dodging Greenies and hovercopters, dealing with*

*absent-father issues, and coming to terms with feelings for an ex-boyfriend—and Jag as a possible new one—leave Vi little time for much else. **(My note: she's got problems. Lots of them.)** Which is too damn bad, because she's more important than she realizes. **(My note: Whoa. She's important? How so?)***

Better keep reading to find out, yo.

And not just the cover copy—but the whole enchilada. One-click buy that book! Right?

Vi's main conflict is that she doesn't know who and/or what she is. How important she is. But everyone else does. And it's not something she's going to like…. This is all established in a mere 42 words.

I also want to point out here that the ex-boyfriend is not named. And he's a huge, massive part of the story. Not only this one, but the entire trilogy. He's not named in the blurb, because it's my job as the author to SELL THE STORY, not make sure I include everything.

In this case, I wanted the agents to request to read my full novel. In our case as Indie authors, we want readers to buy the book now. Read it now. So your job is even more important—and it's to SELL THE STORY.

Not look important.

Not provide all information.

Not be vague.

STOP and WORK:

Think about the book you're working on. My guess is you're far enough into it to know the main conflict. So write it below the tagline, hook, and setup you've been working on so far.

You might find here that you need to name another character for things to make sense. In speculative novels, villains are almost always necessary to put in the blurb. There's usually an outside force the MCs are working against, and you don't want to be Vaguebooking them.

Don't let them take over, but a sentence about who they are and why they're the evil villain they are probably won't hurt.

It's not entirely necessary either.

Let's look at the blurb for Harry Potter and the Sorcerer's Stone:

Harry Potter has never been the star of a Quidditch team, scoring points while riding a broom far above the ground. He knows no spells, has never helped to hatch a dragon, and has never worn a cloak of invisibility. (This is all hook and setup. I actually think the first sentence is the hook. I'm going ooh, Quidditch? I don't know what that is either! Better keep reading.)

All he knows is a miserable life with the Dursleys, his horrible aunt and uncle, and their abominable son, Dudley - a great big swollen spoiled bully. Harry's room is a tiny closet at the foot of the stairs, and he hasn't had a birthday party in eleven years. (This is pure setup. We're learning about Harry. In Indie blurbs, I'd probably nix the formal names of the Dursleys and Dudley, but you know. I'm not JK. But take them out and see if you lose any meaning. I don't think you do.

By the way, that's a great tip. If you have something in your blurb, and you're unsure about it—take it out. My long-time motto for editing has been "When in doubt, delete." It's served me well for many years. It can work in blurb-writing too. If you take out the parts you're not sure of, do you lose meaning? If so, can you rewrite them in a different way so things are more succinct, pushing me toward that final consequence? If so, do that. If you don't lose any meaning, yay! Not needed.)

But all that is about to change when a mysterious letter arrives by owl messenger: a letter with an invitation to an incredible place that Harry - and anyone who reads about him - will find unforgettable. (This is the catalyst to the conflict. He gets a letter to Hogwarts. I want to mention here that this blurb is almost over. Do you know when Harry gets the letters in the book? Chapter 3. THREE. You seriously can write your blurb VERY early in the novel-writing process too. Everything in the blurb generally takes place in the first 25% of the book itself.)

For it's there that he finds not only friends, aerial sports, and magic in everything from classes to meals, but a great destiny that's been waiting for him... (This is the conflict. He's been placed with other humans in an extraordinary situation.) *if Harry can survive the encounter.* (This is the consequence. You'll note that Voldemort is NOT NAMED. Haha. He-who-must-not-be-named! I love that.)

No matter what, your conflict needs to be central to the story and it needs to be summed up in a few sentences in your blurb. It needs to be compelling. This is the last stretch toward the top of the mountain, and it's steep. But you're up to the task.

FINAL WORDS ON THE CONFLICT:

- Find the main conflict and highlight that. Trust me, your blurb—and bottom line—will thank you.
- No novel is complete without conflict. Be sure you identify what the character wants (to find a missing best friend, solve a murder, get a beating heart, fall in love, save a space station, etc.) and then state what or who is keeping them from getting it.
- Don't drag it out. As always, blurb-writing is about being succinct. Take 3-4 sentences if you need them. If you don't, use less.
- Only include vital names and situations that propel the reader to keep reading.

8

WRITING GREAT BLURBS, PART 4: THE CONSEQUENCE

Oh my heck! We're almost there! You've been on this goat for a while now. Starting to get bumpy. Probably. But you started out strong with a tagline and a hook. You made it over the bridge with the troll in the setup. And you've scaled the side of the mountain in the conflict.

Now you're at the top of the mountain and it's time to drop off the passengers and skedaddle.

The final element you need in your query letter is the consequence. What will happen if the MC doesn't solve the problem? Doesn't get what they want? Will evil forces achieve world domination? Will her brother die? Is it a race against time across Antarctica to find the long-lost jewel of the Nile? What's the consequence if you don't come in first?

Through all of my work with other authors on their query letters and blurbs, this is the element that is lacking the most.

The consequence. You've hooked me, set me up, explained the conflict that's keeping me from getting what I want, but...what will happen if I don't solve the conflict? That's the consequence. If you're having trouble identifying yours, it's time to go back to the revising stage—in the novel.

Houston, you have a problem.

And the sooner you know it, the less work you have to do. So once again, see if you can't craft your blurb while you're writing your novel.

The consequence is usually one sentence. In specific genres, I advocate for a strong sentence—no questions. But some genres have questions that are common for that type of book. For example, when I wrote speculative fiction, I used strong statements for my consequences. In romance, the blurbs I've studied often have questions.

There's no "right" or "wrong" here. Other than having a consequence sentence of some kind, that is. You definitely need one of those.

Ask: What's at stake here? And the more personal the stakes are, the better. It's fine to have the entire world hanging in the balance, but what does that have to do with the main character?

If you make it personal to the person you've been telling readers about for the last several sentences, the more likely they are to buy. And if you can make that character as human as possible—like the person buying the book?

Gold.

After all, remember, we ALL want to be heroes.

Let's finish my blurb for that first traditionally published book, and look at the consequence.

In a world where Thinkers brainwash the population and Rules are not meant to be broken, fifteen-year-old Violet Schoenfeld does a hell of a job shattering them to pieces.

After committing her eighth lame ass crime (walking in the park after dark with a boy, gasp!), Vi is taken to the Green, a group of Thinkers who control the Goodgrounds. She's found unrehabilitatable (yeah, she doesn't think it's a word either) and exiled to the Badlands. Good thing sexy Bad boy Jag Barque will be going too.

Dodging Greenies and hovercopters, dealing with absent-father issues, and coming to terms with feelings for an ex-boyfriend—and Jag as a possible new one—leave Vi little time for much else. Which is too damn bad, because she's more important than she realizes. **(Here's where the consequence starts >>)** *When secrets about her "dead" sister and not-so-missing father hit the fan, Vi must make a choice: control or be controlled.*

Oooh, what will it be? You'll have to read to find out...

151 words from beginning to end. And those last 4 words were what made it all the way through all the traditional publishing process and onto the cover of my published book.

That last sentence is the consequence. You need one to complete the blurb and give the reader one final push to buy the book and read it.

You've marched them up the mountain and you're going

to leave them there. That's right. There's no resolution in the blurb—this isn't a synopsis. The blurb should have a cliffhanger, leaving the reader to going, "Oh, that's it. I'm giving up food and sleep until I read this book."

The consequence statement should be just as "hooky" as the hook to leave the reader salivating to read the book. Most consequence hooks tie back to the beginning hook too, for a satisfying circuit in the letter.

Here's this one:

In a world where Thinkers brainwash the population and Rules are not meant to be broken, fifteen-year-old Violet Schoenfeld does a hell of a job shattering them to pieces. When secrets about her "dead" sister and not-so-missing father hit the fan, Vi must make a choice: control or be controlled.

I took out the middle parts, and the blurb still makes sense. When in doubt, delete, right? Yes, right. Often, when you're sending your book out in your newsletters, or applying for ads, they want a shorter blurb than the full thing.

See if you can take the first sentence—the hook—and the last one—the consequence—and have the entire novel summed up. Did it come full circle?

Test Yourself 1: Take the first sentence of your query blurb and copy it into a new document. Now copy and paste your last sentence (your consequence sentence) right behind it. Is that your book? It should be—in a nutshell.

. . .

STOP and WORK:

Take a moment to write a consequence sentence for your current manuscript. You've been working on all the parts during this book. See if you can write just one sentence—and questions are okay—for the consequence.

Answer: What's at stake for my character? If you're writing a romance or a novel with more than one narrating or hugely main character, you might get more than one sentence.

Go look at the blurbs on those books you identified earlier in this book. You know, the ones selling in the Top 50 of the category where your book fits really well.

Tip: Separate the consequence from the rest of the blurb. Is it concise? Does that book even have one? Is it a cliffhanger? Enough to entice you, as the reader, to want to read the entire book?

You'll see some really good examples, and you'll probably see some that could use some work.

Your job is to make yours one of the really good ones. The better every piece of your blurb is, the better your conversion rate will be when you get the right readers to your product page.

Test Yourself 2: Let's look at your own blurbs on your own published books. This is a great exercise to see if you have all the parts that should be present in a blurb. I use the box test to decide if my blurb needs work.

If I can't draw a box around every single sentence and label them as either belonging to the hook, the setup, the conflict, or the consequence, that sentence or bit of information needs to go. Stat.

So I do that test for all blurbs—existing and new ones. If I can't identify where a sentence or a phrase goes into the formula, I don't need it or I need to rewrite it.

FINAL WORDS ON THE CONFLICT:

- Leave the reader on a "cliffhanger"—needing to buy the book and read now to find out what happens.
- Use a strong statement or a compelling question as your departing remark.
- Bring the blurb full-circle, tying your beginning hook to your cliffhanger consequence.

9

EVERYTHING ELSE

O kay, so you made it through the parts of an amazing blurb! I hope you learned something along the way, and that it had more to do with writing an amazing piece of work you can use to sell your books and less with goats or *The Bachelorette*.

Okay, maybe not that last one. ;)

Now that you have an amazing blurb, you're going to run it by Your Person. Or People. Get some feedback on it and see if you've hit all the high points.

Change it up on the retailers if it's a live book, and then...wait. Don't expect your conversions to suddenly double overnight. But if you are running ads to the book in question, I would think that you should be able to see some improvement in a week or two.

The important thing to do is keep track. This can be as

simple as using a Google Sheet and putting in a few simple numbers.

For the period 2 weeks before you changed the blurb, note:

1. Number of sales and pagereads
2. Number of clicks it took to get those
3. Ad spend

You calculate your conversion by taking how many sales you got and divide it by the number of clicks it took to get those. For example, let's say I sold 500 books over a 2-week period. And it took 2000 clicks to do that. That's a conversion rate of 25%, which is actually really good.

I strive to have at least 20%, but I'm actually happy with 10%. Sometimes less, if the book is full price.

Then I see how much I spent to make those sales, but I don't do much with it here. You can, but that's not what this book is about.

After 2 weeks with the new blurb, do the same thing. Note the sales and pagereads and the number of clicks from your ads. Recalculate the conversion.

If it's gone up, yay! Your blurb is working. If not, you have a couple of choices. You can try a new tagline—the text above the fold on Amazon, specifically. You can examine your cover and decide if it's to-market enough.

You can look at your ads and decide if they're really doing what you want them to. The biggest problem with all the moving parts of Indie publishing and advertising is determining which cog will help us sell more books.

I personally think killer cover copy will help you sell more books, but you might not be able to tell after just a couple of weeks.

So the first part of Everything Else is don't panic. It might take some time to really see your blurb increasing your conversions. You can't control everything, but what you can, you should. And your blurb is one of those things.

I've already mentioned the Kindlepreuner description tool, but that's definitely part of the Everything Else I use. I actually code mine with HTML, but the tool does a good job if you don't know the codes. I think having a bolded tagline improves the blurb, because it draws the eye.

There's an eye study I read a while ago on Joanna Penn's website. It was an eye-tracking study of people looking at an Amazon product page. They spend a lot of time looking at the cover, and the bigger, bolder title, subtitle, and series title. This was obvious to me.

And on one of the images, I saw that there was also a hotspot on the tagline area. And putting that in bold, or caps, or both, could really help me sell my books.

I've also experimented with making this tagline a head-line, which means bigger text. I've done a Headline 3, which isn't that huge. I don't like it as much, because it's literally the only thing I can see above the See More button, whereas

I didn't see much difference between that and just a regular-sized, bolded tagline.

And they can see the beginning of my hook with the regular-sized tagline, so I don't use that much anymore.

But hey, if there's anything I advocate for Indies, it's to test everything for yourself. Remember that chapter earlier where I talked about me, me, *me*? Yeah, that. Test for yourself and see what happens.

Just be sure to give it enough time. Sometimes I think there are monkeys running the algorithms at Amazon, and they're not always trained. Haha! So give things time to settle and work—or not work—before you make a decision.

Oh, and if you want to see that eye study, you can go here.

I'm a strong advocate of using my description box to really use more keywords. I don't stuff illegally, but I try to put in things that I think will help me show up in searches. Amazon allows this, as long as you're not referencing another author or another book—that's against their Terms of Service.

So I always put in some other general stuff. Here's an example:

Escape to Getaway Bay and join the Clean Billionaire Beach Club for some seriously sweet romance.

Each book can be read as a standalone, with a happily-ever-after ending, and clean, sweet-without-losing-the-heat romance!

So I've put in some CTAs here that are using keywords.

Sweet romance. Happily-ever-after. Clean. Billionaire. Getaway Bay. Etc.

So I usually have some sort of general statements that act as calls-to-action within the blurb. They are always beneath the consequence statement, after the blurb.

And I've been using the rest of my product description space to list my series and titles. I put in that I'm a USA Today bestseller. All of these are search terms, and I want to show up in searches for any of my books, no matter what a customer is searching.

So that's another part of the Everything Else I do in the product description box.

STOP and WORK:

Make a plan for your new blurb. Prepare your previous 2 weeks worth of data, and then put in your shiny new blurb and...forget about it. Ha! But no, give it some time.

Come back to it in 2 weeks and hope the monkeys have been trained by then.

FINAL WORDS ON EVERYTHING ELSE:

- Don't panic.
- Make your tagline bold. I forgot to say that I almost always bold my consequence sentence in my blurbs too. Just to draw the eye.

- Check out the description tools to make your taglines and blurbs pretty.
- Use the space in your description box for more keyword possibilities.
- Don't be afraid to make changes if you don't see the results you want.
- Test, test, test.

10

CREATING COPY FOR ADS

Now that you have an amazing, shiny, working blurb, it's time to get more eyeballs on your product page. More people buying and reading your book.

You do this by advertising, of course, and that comes in many different formats and strategies.

You can use your awesome copy in all types of ads, including Amazon, Facebook, and BookBub. True, BookBub only allows images, but you can put your tagline—or part of it—on the image you use. Don't clutter up the image with too much text, though. That's a big no-no in BookBub paid advertising.

Facebook allows you to put in a lot of words, and you can test entire blurbs there. Amazon is the most restrictive in terms of length, only allowing 150 characters. There are several strategies where I've used my cover copy in my ad copy.

I've done checklists with the tropes. I've used my final consequence question. I've used my tagline. I've used my generic statements at the end of my descriptions.

The point is, you can use any of those things you've just spent this book working on. So the work you've been doing on your blurb can now do double-duty. And as you're testing each piece through advertising, see which ones are producing the best results.

One note here: Don't start 5 ads at the same time, testing 5 different things, for the same book. If you do that, you will not be able to tell WHICH ad is producing any extra sales.

You have to go slow when testing blurbs, copy, and taglines. One ad at a time. Don't change anything but the copy. Compare results once the tests are done. You can choose to use the ad that got the most clicks, though sometimes the clickiest ads aren't the ones that convert the best.

You can keep track of the conversion for Ad 1 and compare it to Ad 2, where the only difference is the copy used. Which one produced more conversions? That's the winning copy, and you can use that in your product description box too.

Remember, you don't know what you don't know. You might have amazing ideas. Work really hard and write an awesome blurb using all the steps and tips in this book...and it still might not convert.

Always test. Let the clickers/readers tell you which copy to use.

I believe, and I've seen from my own experience over the past twelve years, that cover copy that has all the things I've laid out in this book converts the best.

Having tight, compelling copy that propels a reader to the end of the blurb and leaves them wanting more produces more sales than vague, wandering, text-heavy descriptions. Don't be afraid of white space in your blurbs. We have to breathe going up that mountain, you know?

So get down to business, and get your blurbs shined up. Start testing them. Start selling more books.

11

WRAPPING UP!

H oly starfish, Batman! That was a lot, wasn't it? I know it was. But hopefully you bought the book, and you can come back to it anytime you want. Make notes. Make some more. Rewrite your blurbs. Box up those sentences and make sure they're working for you. March people up the hill and then throw the goat off the cliff.

Wait. Don't do that last part. No goats should be harmed in the writing of your blurbs.

Don't be overwhelmed. Writing a blurb or ad copy is something you *can* do. You *can* become good at it. It's a skill you *can* learn.

One of the most important lessons I've learned as I read Facebook groups, study courses, and read book like this is that you can easily overwhelm yourself with the information.

It's broken down for you, one part at a time. Take five days and write a new part of your new blurb each day. Go slow. Don't feel like you've done everything wrong up until now and you better fix it before the sky falls!

Trust me, I've felt that panic. And you know what I do instead?

There's this little thing called...*The Bachelorette*.

LOL.

The point is, don't stress out to the point where you can't work at all. Just make a plan for yourself and your existing blurbs and move forward with it, one step at a time.

I hope you feel inspired to take control of your cover copy and really make it shine. There is a lot out there to make an Indie author's life easier. There are a lot of people around to help. I hope you'll join me on Facebook on my Indie Inspiration page, where I post content at least three times a week for Indie authors in all stages of their careers.

You can also find the videos on my YouTube channel. And I'll be sending out content in my Indie Inspiration newsletter for authors too. Join!

Hopefully, you feel excited about the next stage of your career, and hopefully you've learned something about how to make your product page convert into more sales for you.

FINAL THOUGHTS:

Do three things now:

1. Plan to write the blurb for the book you're writing right now. Notice I didn't say go write the blurb right now. I said plan to write the blurb. Just put it on your to-do list for some time in say, the next week.
2. Choose an existing blurb. Copy and paste it into a new document and print it. Do the box test on it, and draw a box around every sentence, assigning it one of the parts of a killer blurb.
3. Take a deep breath and eat something you love. I'm going to go get a pepperoni pizza.

Good luck out there! And don't forget, you can find the PDF to help you organize your thoughts as you work on your blurb on the Writing Killer Cover Copy resources page.

———

I hope you learned something in this book! My Indie Inspiration catalog has another book—**WRITING AND RELEASING RAPIDLY**. It's filled with writing and releasing strategies, where I share real data and peel back the curtain on everything marketing I've done over the past several years. **GO GRAB IT today! It's available in Kindle Unlimited too.**

If you enjoyed this book, **please leave a review**!

Writing and Releasing Rapidly (Book 1): You've heard the term "Rapid Release" and you're wondering if it's a viable strategy for you. This book has everything you need to get started writing and releasing quicker, as well as half a dozen case studies outlining 6 different Rapid Release Launches Elana has tried for herself.

BOOKS IN THE INDIE INSPIRATION LINE

Writing Killer Cover Copy (Book 2): Craft cover copy that will convert browsers into buyers at a higher rate, entice readers to buy *and* read immediately, and sell more books!

ABOUT ELANA

Elana Johnson is the USA Today bestselling author of dozens of novels, from YA contemporary romance to adult beach romances. Check out her beach romance in the Hawthorne Harbor Romance series, the Clean Beach Club Billionaire Romance series, the Beaches & Brides Romance series, the Stranded in Paradise Romance series, and the Forbidden Lake Romance series.

She also writes as Liz Isaacson, the USA Today Bestselling and Kindle Unlimited All-Start Author of the #1 bestselling Three Rivers Ranch Romance series, the #1 bestselling Horseshoe Home Ranch Romance series, the Brush Creek Brides series, the USA Today bestselling Steeple Ridge Romance series (Buttars Brothers novels), the Grape Seed Falls Romance series, the Christmas in Coral Canyon Romance series (Whittaker Brothers novels), the Quinn Valley Ranch Romance series, and the Last Chance Ranch Romance series.

If you liked this book, please take a few minutes to leave a review now! Authors (Elana included!) really appreciate this, and it helps draw more readers to books they might like. Thanks!